Contents

The support of the Calouste Gulbenkian Foundation is gratefully acknowledged.

Editors: Paul Quin and Geoff Worthington

Published by the John Pounds of Portsmouth Heritage Appeal January 2007

Graphic Design by AW Solutions, Portsmouth

Cover picture: John Pounds in his Cobbler's Workshop teaching 'his' children.
From an original by H S Sheaf made in 1838.

ISBN 978 0 9554990 0 5

Foreword

This book is a tribute to John Pounds (1766 -1839) whose life and times are well chronicled here and to the Reverend John Sturges, two men of Portsmouth who shared a devotion to the care and education of others, to justice and to their faith.

Following the loss of the original Portsmouth High Street Chapel in 1941 John Sturges pioneered its re-building after the War and renamed it the John Pounds Memorial Church. He was Minister Emeritus at the time of his death in 1998 and was working tirelessly to achieve another goal which he held dearly – to have a replica of the original John Pounds workshop created.

Today the remains of both men, John Sturges & John Pounds, lie within the churchyard close to that replica of the workshop, which was completed in 2004 and today forms a symbolic link to their achievements.

In this publication we are privileged to have essays of individual scholarship accompanying the original John Sturges text covering the life and work of John Pounds. Dr. Ann Coats brings to our attention some facts never previously published following her study of dockyard records at The National Archives. Elizabeth Barnes-Downing has provided a two-part feature on Portsmouth and life in general at the time of John Pounds which sets in context his contributions. Professor Tony Pointon, Emeritus Professor of Portsmouth University and Chairman of the University Dickens Fellowship, explores answers to the questions: "Did Charles Dickens and John Pounds ever meet?" and "What influence did the life's work of Pounds have on Dickens?"

We aspire to continue to inform and educate our community, particularly school children, about John Pounds and the examples of humility and love he so clearly demonstrated. Further, to provide practical assistance to young people via donations to help them towards personal goals which they might not otherwise achieve.

Your support in buying this book is helping us towards these aims. Thank-you.

Geoff Worthington
Chairman, John Pounds of Portsmouth Heritage Appeal
Member John Pounds Trust

Portsmouth in the time of John Pounds (1766 -1839)

Part 1 by Elizabeth Barnes-Downing

A view across Southsea Common towards the town, circa 1800. Picture courtesy of Portsmouth Museums & Records Service.

Portsmouth was a walled garrison town until the 1870s, occupying a small area on the south-western corner of Portsea Island. The walls and ramparts were largely earth embankments with mature elm trees growing on them. The first census of 1801 recorded the population at 33,226, by far the largest urban centre in the county of Hampshire. Southampton, second largest town in Hampshire, supported a population one quarter of that size. There was a diverse social mix – from the gentry and middle-classes, who lived in the fine houses along the top of the High Street, the merchants in their high class shops further down this street; the sailors passing through the port; the prostitutes who tapped into this passing trade; and at the bottom of the socio-economic ladder, the deprived and wretched who inhabited cramped and squalid rooms in the narrow courtyards, rat-runs and alleys leading from the back streets.

These backstreets and courts were also used to keep pigs. In one example, between twenty and thirty pigs were kept in a confined space behind dwellings in East

Picture courtesy of Portsmouth in the Past.

Street, and the stench certainly did not pass unnoticed - in fact it was reported that at times residents were forced to leave their homes to escape the 'pestiferous' smell.[1]

In the streets, particularly Broad Street and the notorious Point, press gangs took able-bodied men away from their families unless powerful reasons (or bribes) enabled their release. Royal Naval seamen of all ranks received pay only after a ship had been decommissioned, which could be several years. Families left behind had to find other means to get by in the meantime or be left destitute, swelling the numbers in the town dependent upon poor relief.

Death and disabling injury at sea were commonplace: disease and accidents took more lives than shipwreck and fighting – HM Royal Navy figures for 1810 confirm that a startling 80% of fatalities were from the former causes.[2] By way of compensation, pensions for widows and their families were limited. Money for families affected by shipwreck would be raised by public subscription, but amounts were variable and dependent upon the size of the disaster's profile. Disasters at sea capturing the public's imagination would attract larger collections than 'lesser' events, even though the sufferings of the families would be of equal magnitude. Eligibility was acknowledged by social legitimacy - families of the common law service wife would be overlooked.

Many hundreds of children were orphaned or abandoned through death, disease, transportation or other family disasters.

Broad Street. Picture courtesy of Portsmouth in the Past.

Portsea Island 1833

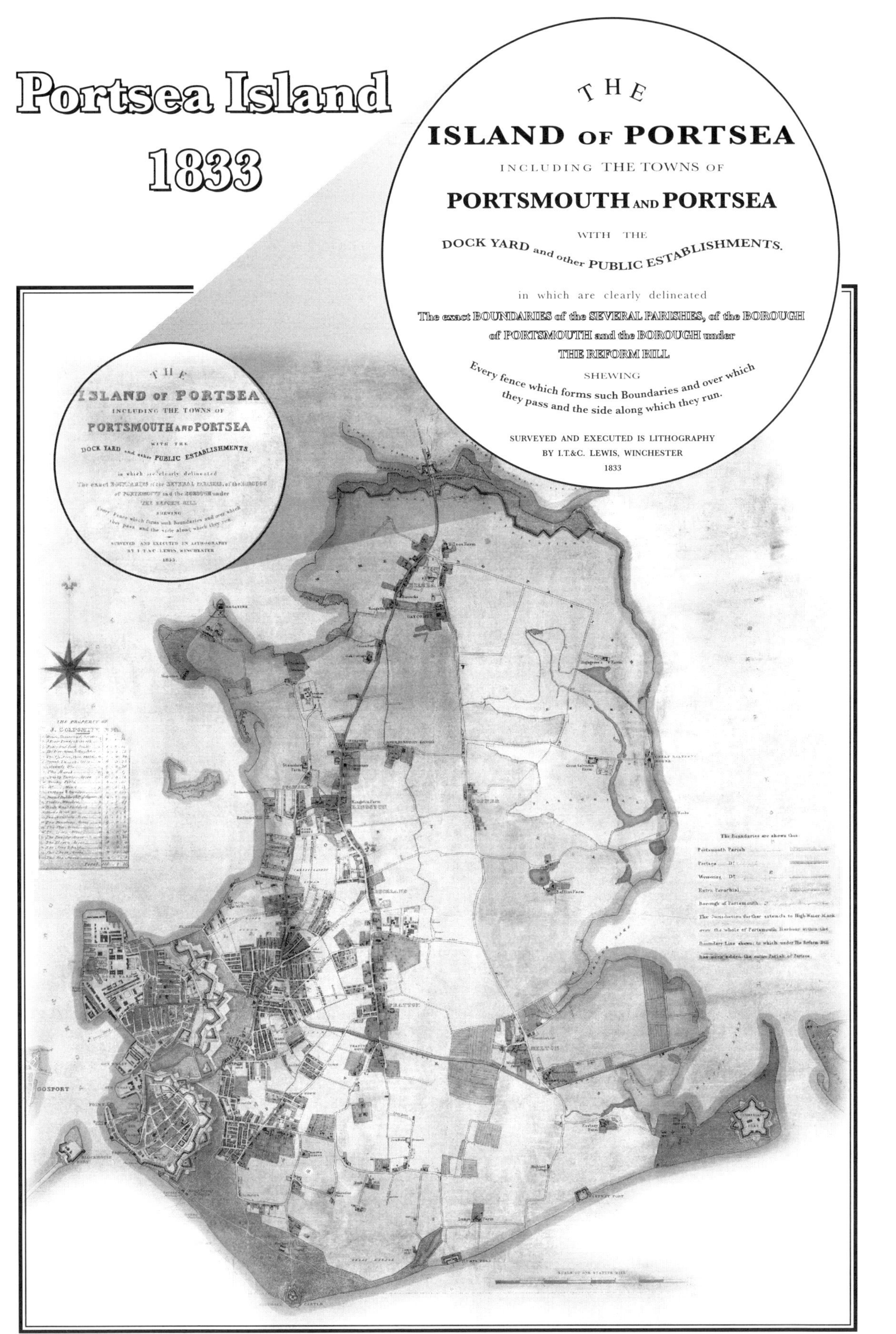

Picture courtesy of Portsmouth Museums & Records Service.

The Plight of the Children.

St. Mary's Street... of the seventy-four houses, seven are occupied by licensed victuallers, sixteen are beer houses, fourteen are licensed refreshment houses, five are private brothels, whilst nearly all the houses in the many courts and alleys adjoining are rented by beer-house keepers and let in rooms to the unfortunate wretches who frequent their vile dens....one scoundrel had the audacity to call his house the 'Infant School'.
Letter to the Hampshire Telegraph (1866)
From The Portsmouth Papers No.38, page 12.

Ragged Schools were for : " Children convicts who have been transport children of thieves not in custody; child of worthless drunken parents; orpha deserted children and runaways who by begging and stealing".

In the early 1800s, the State contribution to education was less than the amount the Government spent on the King's stables.

" ...a vast hopeless nursery of ignorance, misery and vice: a breeding place for the hulks and jails...the very sweepings of the streets.... with nothing frank, ingenious or pleasant in their faces, low-browed vicious, cunning, wicked; abandoned of all help...so discarded by all social teachers but the gaoler and the hangman.."
Charles Dickens
A plea for the support of Ragged Schools
Letter to The Daily News

William Sivier had twenty previous convictions for vagrancy and theft when he appeared in court accused of obtaining money by false pretences (pretending to be orphaned by the cholera epidemic) at the age of twelve.
The Portsmouth Papers No.21, page 7.

"Such was Messum's Court... reached from Prospect Row an through a tunnel only two feet wid which was called Squeeze Gu Alley. Here 116 people lived, som in cellars, with one privy betwee them and one standpipe whic supplied water for ten minutes day"
The Portsmouth Papers No.21, page 3.

the sweepings of the streets"

'This young girl patient's workroom lay only seven feet from an open cesspool which received blood and washings from a pig-killing establishment where the smell was so pestiferous that I could not remain five minutes without fainting."
Dr. Engledue
Founder of the Royal Portsmouth Hospital
The Portsmouth Papers No.21, page 4.

"In the hovels of Matrimony Row and the dens of Jacob's Ladder with their walls half a brick thick and their eight feet by six kitchens slopping with liquid filth, the wretched inhabitants often shared a bed of rags and straw between three or four.
The Portsmouth Papers No.21, page 4.

Court report....Samuel Egdon (13) and Richard Lovett (15) guilty of stealing 6oz tobacco and a bottle of ginger beer - sentence 12 months imprisonment and a whipping; the brothers Pickett, aged 11 and 13 guilty of throwing stones at a door – sentence fourteen days hard labour.
The Portsmouth Papers No.55, page 11.

the boy had " neither shoes nor stockings: his naked feet are red, swollen, cracked, ulcerated with the cold."
Dr. Thomas Guthrie

Almost every week there were reports in the Hampshire Telegraph of them (children) falling into fires, pulling pans of boiling water over themselves or setting their clothing alight. They fell into the uncovered wells, drowned themselves clambering over the logs in the water at the Hard or were maimed or killed under the wheels of vehicles or the flying hooves of horses.
The Portsmouth Papers No.21, page 6.

..Portsmouth is not only filthy and crowded, ut crowded with a class of low and abandoned ings, who seem to have declared war against ery habit of common decency and decorum ...... re hordes of profligate females are seen reeling drunkenness or plying upon the streets in open y with a broad immodesty, which puts the great b of noon to blush."
r. George Pinckard (1795)
e Portsmouth Papers No. 20, page 7.

" ...half-famished, half-naked children who prowl about alleys and railway-arches, fruit markets and the river shore...."
Thomas Barnardo

The Life & Work of John Pounds (1766 -1839)

From the original text by The Reverend John Sturges

A Local Hero

Portsmouth people have long regarded John Pounds as one of their heroes. For generations they had visited his cobbler's shop in St. Mary's Street Old Portsmouth, to see the place where he had "educated, clothed and fed" hundreds of youngsters over many years. For nearly a century, until it was removed circa 1940 children were taken to the workshop to hear the story of John Pounds. In recent years they have come to visit the memorial stone in the John Pounds Memorial Church's Garden in the High Street where he was buried and they also continue to hear of the work he did long before schools existed for most children, so that there is still a lively appreciation of this local personality.

For them, he was a good man who, for the greater part of his life, cared for the neglected children who once roamed the narrow streets and alleys of the old town. They knew that his practical goodness had influenced many people, including some famous reformers, so that they too began to be concerned for the needs of such children. Many similar schools grew up in the larger towns and cities throughout the country, and Portsmouth people are rightly proud that their local hero, who had lived and worked in comparative obscurity, has now come to be recognised as a pioneer of popular education.

The Early Years

John Pounds was born in Portsmouth on the 17th June 1766, the son of a sawyer who worked in the Royal Dockyard. At 12 years of age he too went to work there as a shipwright apprentice, but after some 2 years he met with an accident and was badly crippled for the rest of his life. He had fallen down into a dry dock and although he recovered, his back was bent double and he was badly deformed.

It was a gloomy prospect for a youngster, especially as most jobs were for manual workers, either in the Royal Dockyard, the various Government victualling yards and stores or the local brewery. The long period of recovery was spent in reading and in educating himself. He had a quick and alert intelligence and was interested in a wide variety of subjects. Moreover, once he began to walk again, his natural vitality asserted itself and he was often to be seen walking the fortifications or on Portsmouth Common and then further afield to Wymering fields, Portsdown Hill or Havant Thicket.

He was interested in natural history and had a keen eye for all the details of the natural world of flowers, plants and wildlife. He was endowed with a powerful physique and a healthy disposition so that the years of recuperation were a fruitful time for his physical and mental development. It is certainly not true that he was a pale pathetic invalid. He was a strong and intelligent man who, although badly crippled, had learned to cope with his disability and lived an active life.

However a man must earn some sort of living and he became a cobbler making and mending shoes for the people of the neighbourhood. One summer he was employed as a cook on a ship bringing stone from Swanage for the construction of the Gunwharf Wall at Portsmouth. Then he returned to his cobbling, working for a number of employers and eventually setting up his own cobbler's shop. That was how he earned his living for the rest of his life, and when he died at the age of 72 he was still repairing boots and shoes.

The Cobbler's Shop

Of course, Portsmouth was a very busy place. The wars saw the Dockyard crowded with ships and the streets full of soldiers and sailors. There were the French prisoners in the hulks in Portsmouth and Langstone Harbours and the convicts awaiting transportation, engaged on Government works outside the town. There must have been plenty of work for a cobbler and it was said that, at one time, John earned as much as a guinea a week which was nearly double what he would have been paid in the Dockyard or in the Brewery. By 1803 "the year of the invasion scare" he had saved enough to buy the place which became his living accommodation and

Picture courtesy of Portsmouth Museums & Records Service.

workshop and where he lived and worked for the rest of his life. It was in the same street where he had been born and where he had grown up, known as St. Mary's Street and later renamed Highbury Street.

It was a modest building, little more than a shed. It had been erected using the two walls of adjoining properties. It had a weather boarded front and back and a tiled roof. There were two rooms, one upstairs serving as a bedroom, and the downstairs room was used as both a living room and a workshop. The frontage was only seven feet, the depth from the front to the back some sixteen feet and the rooms some six feet in height. But this tiny, modest place had a frontage onto the street with a window at which John Pounds sat at his bench mending his shoes. It had a stable door, the top half of which was usually open so that people passing could see and speak to John Pounds at his work.

Picture courtesy of Barnardo's Image Archive

In fact it was a very busy street with people passing by all the time. Although it was a long narrow street, it led to the gate through the fortifications and was the main route from Portsmouth to the Mill Pond and across Portsmouth Common to the Hard. Hundreds of people must have passed by the cobbler's shop and many must have discussed with him the affairs of the community. This was the place where he lived for the rest of his life and where, whilst earning his living as a cobbler, he was to educate so many poor children of the neighbourhood.

It is ironic that John Pounds, a bachelor all his life probably due to his deformity, should have played such an enormous role in the lives of children then and since. He was first set on his path by the tragic circumstances of his nephew, Johnny, who was born with both feet turned inwards.

Hearing that the very young boy was due to have his ankles broken, a crude and dangerous operation in those days, John Pounds asked to be allowed to look after the youngster. His sister was only too pleased to grant the request.

Once in his care, John Pounds set about rectifying his nephew's disability, making one of the earliest pairs of orthopaedic boots. By adjusting the width of the leather gradually, although painful for the boy, the legs were straightened to normality. He went on to perform similar feats for many other afflicted children over the years.

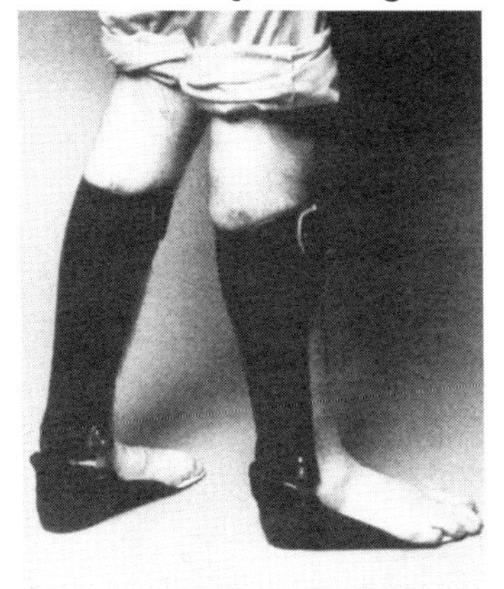
Later corrective footwear

As soon as the youth was fully mobile, his uncle set about finding Johnny some playmates, first of all consulting his friend and benefactor, Edward Carter, manager of Pike's Brewery - a step that was to lead to the Ragged School movement.

His nephew would eventually follow him into the trade and take over the tiny workshop and living area following the sudden death of John Pounds in 1839.

Already something of a character, John and his cobbler's shop became a focus of interest for many poor people and the children came to him from the courts and alleys of that crowded area of Portsmouth. Nearby was the Camber where the trading vessels loaded and unloaded their cargoes. There were the great government stores, the rope works and, near to The Hard, were the shallow basins where the logs were being seasoned.

So the area was crowded with activities. Poor people and destitute children congregated in these places, hoping to find food and shelter. John knew many of them from his boyhood days. He knew their families and he knew the sad circumstances which had rendered them destitute. Although he had a reputation as a rough and somewhat uncouth character of sturdy independence, he seemed to have a natural sympathy for people in need and a ready resourcefulness which enabled him to be of help to them. He came to be known as a man who could be relied upon to do something for them. If it was footwear needing repair or someone needing a meal, or a child with some sickness or injury, then John would, in his own rough fashion, try and find some way of helping them. Everything that affected the life of that community was his concern.

The fact that his cobbler's shop was in the middle of one of the main thoroughfares, and that he usually had the top half of his front door open, meant that he was in a unique position to discover what was happening, often before others in the neighbourhood. All sorts of people, some very influential such as solicitors, Dockyard officials and Aldermen, passed his shop and he often engaged them in conversation. He would put to them direct questions and although he did not always get a direct reply, it was usually sufficient to give him some idea of what was happening.

He often knew of discharges from the Dockyard or the disposal of the property of well known persons long before it was common knowledge and, in the days when people did not read newspapers, he became a valuable source of information.

His friend Frank Faulkner, who drove The Rocket from Portsmouth to London, would call in on him and pass on "intelligence from London". Another friend, Lemmon, the master of a trading vessel, would bring him scraps of news - so the cobbler's shop was the place where people gathered to find out the news of the day. The year 1803, when he moved into his cobbler's shop, was the year of a threatened invasion and one can imagine how everyone thirsted for news.

As a man of education, he would often be asked to read letters from abroad to parents who could not themselves read and no doubt he would offer to write a reply. Private correspondence must have been a most valuable channel of information and made him almost indispensable in that small community. John became one of the personalities of the area and people looked to him as their natural leader. He was a familiar figure to them as he made his way to the town gates and fortifications at early morning or at sunset. Because of his deformity, he always used a stick for walking and because of its metal tip, he could usually be heard as he made his way through the streets and alleys.

There were others who were irresistibly drawn to his cobbler's shop - particularly the destitute youngsters of the area. Many of these were orphans, their fathers having been lost at sea and their mothers dead from cholera or some other prevalent disease. With these children he was always kind and helpful. He had infinite patience, was full of fascinating information and always ready with a story. He seemed to know exactly what would arouse their interest and hold their attention. Perhaps it was the birds, recovering from injuries in cages in the workshop and the other pets that attracted them to his workshop. Sometimes it was because they were hungry and needed something to eat but, whatever the reason, they congregated around him and looked on him as their friend and provider of nourishment for both body and mind.

The Workshop School

It is likely that his school grew out of this friendship with such children; he did not set out to organise a school. There was no precise moment when he made the decision to teach. It was simply that these youngsters got into the habit of going to his little workshop, especially in the cold weather. He naturally captured their interest so that they became willing students. They loved to watch him at work as he handled the leather and used his tools and even while he did his work he found it easy to teach them. If their interest flagged and they became noisy and unruly, then he would assert himself and his instructions would change direction. Then it was time to get out the slates and do the sums - sometimes he would send them out on short journeys of exploration.

His friend, The Reverend Russell Scott, Minister of what was then called the High Street Chapel (now John Pounds Memorial Church since it was rebuilt after the bombing in World War II) had supplied him with bibles, testaments and other reading material. Others had given him slates. He had been given a couple of forms and a number of boxes so that there was somewhere for the children to sit and learn while he was busy with his work. He had a big fire and always there was a large kettle of water boiling away. So the school seemed to develop naturally out of his concern for these youngsters whom "nobody cared for" and who found his little workshop a haven of warmth.

Of course, he was a born teacher. No one could have held their interest unless he had real skill linked to a passionate love of learning and of humanity especially as, most of the time, he was repairing boots and shoes. Very soon this school became the central interest of his life and he did everything he could to make it successful.

He collected clothes from his friends because he was appalled at the children's dirty clothes. He knew that they were often hungry and somehow he managed to provide meals. What he earned he spent on the children and when this was not enough he borrowed from his more affluent friends, constantly explaining that it was "all for the children". He was never backward in asking when something was needed for them. If it was a bandage or ointment or some other necessity, John knew where he could obtain it. Nor did he worry overmuch that his cobbler's shop was so small. They simply crowded around him sitting on the boxes or on the stairs or, if needs be, on the floor.

Sometimes he would go looking for the most neglected. With hot potatoes in his pocket he would find these youngsters hanging around The Camber, or perched on the rafts of logs seasoning in the shallow basins by The Hard. He would toss a potato baked in its jacket and still warm into the cold hands of a boy with the words "there are plenty more where that one came from" knowing that he would be followed home and that he had captured another recruit. It is said that he had sewed extra pockets on to his jacket so that he could put baked tatties in them in order to keep himself warm on cold days. They probably did not stay in the pockets for long when the hungry youngsters and others were around.

It is difficult for us today to imagine what a remarkable step John Pounds took in collecting these neglected and deprived children into his workshop. Every large town had hundreds of such children living in awful conditions in the streets and who were often prey to all the social evils of the day. Perhaps Portsmouth, a major port and a city of transient population, had more than its share.

Hungry, ill clad, often diseased and never washed, they roamed the streets in the day, becoming recruits in their very earliest years into the underclass which frequented the gin shops and taverns. As thieves, cheats and pickpockets they regularly risked incarceration in the convict hulks in Portsmouth harbour and eventual transportation to Botany Bay.

It was well known by the authorities that the adult criminal classes thrived on the efforts of these, often unwilling, youngsters. Social reformers suggested that education might be the answer to, quite literally, keep them off the streets and turn their minds to other more wholesome matters. But how could they be persuaded to turn away from the only lives they knew in favour of an education which, in those days, was only available to those who could pay for it.

The Pickett brothers, aged 11 and 13 years sentenced to 14 days hard labour for throwing stones at a door: Picture courtesy of Portsmouth Museums & Records Service.

In the early years of the nineteenth century the State contribution to education was less than the amount spent by the government on the King's stables!

John Pounds had the answer in his pocket with his enticing jacket potatoes and the will in his heart to follow it through. He is acknowledged to have taken the first steps along the road towards universal free education, later pioneered by Dr. Thomas Guthrie in Scotland and the Seventh Earl of Shaftesbury, leading to child care and protection legislation which would transform society's attitude to children.

The Outdoor School

A surprising feature of the school was its outdoor activities. John believed in the beneficial effects of fresh air and country walks. On fine days the workshop would be closed and he and the children would be off on some excursion. Sometimes they would skirt the fortifications around the town and make their way to the seashore. At other times they went further afield, botanizing and enjoying the countryside. Far beyond the old town were the fields at Wymering and further still was Portsdown Hill - the great ridge of the South Downs overlooking Portsmouth. Westwards along the downs they would go as far as the famous Nelson Monument and, in the opposite direction, they would go to Havant Thicket where highwaymen had been active.

Along the way, the children would be busy collecting flowers, listening for bird calls, identifying trees and spotting insects. From the top of Portsdown Hill they could see the great spread of the two harbours of Portsmouth and Langstone. Below, were

View from Portsdown Hill, 1863. Picture courtesy of Portsmouth Museums & Records Service.

the stone walls and bastions of Portchester Castle. What tales John would tell of the Romans sailing up the Harbour to establish their encampment. He would tell of the arrival of the Normans and the building of the magnificent Keep and Priory Church. Within recent memory he would tell of the Castle crowded with French prisoners and the many attempted escapes.

On a very clear day John would point beyond the harbour to Spithead and the Isle of Wight. To the east they could see the great Cathedral at Chichester. Another splendid view was to the north where they could see the Forest of Bere which had once supplied the oaks for the Navy's "wooden walls". The whole area was full of interest and provided plenty of scope for John's teaching skills.

Along the way, they would stop at some cottage for refreshments. The journey home, a distance of some miles, presented problems for the weary youngsters and they would ride on John's back in spite of his deformity. The coachman, Frank Faulkner, a close friend of John's, immaculate on the seat of the Rocket, would stop and give a couple of the youngsters a seat on the box beside him. As they eventually made their way through the Landport Gate and along the High Street, friends would know that John and the rest of the children were on their way and a meal would be got ready to welcome them.

Sundays too were special. John now always attended the High Street Chapel for worship largely because its Minister, The Reverend Russell Scott, had so generously supported the school. All would meet at the workshop for a meal, then, dressed in the smart clothes he had collected, they would accompany John to the service. For some it must have seemed the highlight of the week.

A True Friend

High Street Chapel

It is not surprising that John became something of a legend in Portsmouth. Everyone seemed to know him and his children and the work he did for them and for everyone that needed his help. Of course, the people of his neighbourhood regarded him as their friend. Many others admired him and were glad to count him as a friend.

Many influential people knew him and were interested in his school. Yet throughout his life he remained independent. He was glad when they asked after the children and particularly pleased when they took a special interest in one of his youngsters and he was delighted when they came with some useful gift. Nothing gave him greater pleasure than to show such people some special accomplishment of one of his scholars. But always he was respectfully independent.

Such people often wondered how he could go on. He always seemed strong and healthy - full of vigour and vitality, but he was no longer a young man and was in his seventies. He had been so badly crippled throughout his life and that must have imposed a strain on him. Some people said he looked tired and when they inquired he always said, "Don't worry, one day I will fall like a bird from its perch" and so he did.

On New Year's Day 1839 one of his boys needed some ointment and John took himself off to the house of Edward Carter at No. 19 the High Street. He was one of John's most influential friends, a wealthy man who had been six times Mayor of

Portsmouth. John was shown into the Hall but, while he was waiting for Edward Carter to attend to him, he suddenly collapsed, fell to the floor and never recovered. George Martell, one of the finest surgeons in Portsmouth was called but he could do little for him and there was nothing for it but to break the sad news to the children waiting for him in his cobbler's shop. They were distraught, for John Pounds had become everything to them: friend, family, teacher, nurse and protector.

When they came to clear up his workshop they found very little. His tools, some leather, the children's books and slates, his store of clothes, the birds and his pets and a jug of sprats for the midday meal. The meagre accumulation of a lifetime of work and service was a measure of his generosity and devotion. All he had ever had was spent on the children and the people of the neighbourhood.

The Carter House, 19 The High Street where John Pounds died

A Memorial to John Pounds

News of his death could have been the end of the story, but it was not. Practical goodness often lingers in the memories of those who were beneficiaries and then it fades and is forgotten within a generation or so. Strangely, that did not happen after John Pounds had died. Of course, news of his death aroused considerable interest and hundreds attended his funeral.

Some of his friends who belonged to the Chapel had thought that some expression of appreciation of his work was needed and a memorial plaque was placed in the Chapel on the wall near his pew. An obituary notice appeared in the local newspaper, and an account of his work found its way into several London newspapers. Brent Price, a printer in the High Street who had long been an admirer, wrote a pamphlet "A Memoir of the late John Pounds of Portsmouth shoemender and gratuitous Teacher of Poor Children" and most of this was reprinted as an article in "The Christian Reformer" of 1839. Such notices stimulated interest in John Pounds and people came to see his grave and one planted a laurel tree nearby.

The nephew, whom John had adopted and trained as a shoemaker, took over the shoe repairing, He had a new shop front put in and soon there was a stream of people wanting to see the little cobbler's shop.

A fund was established which enabled the Memorial Stone to be placed on his grave and can still be seen as the central feature of the Memorial Garden.
Perhaps the most appropriate memorial was the fact that several schools sprang up in different parts of the town. These schools spread to other parts of England and Scotland and so, eventually, the Ragged School Movement was established and hundreds of schools sprang up in the large towns.

The driving force behind the movement was Dr. Thomas Guthrie of Edinburgh. His interest was aroused by a picture of John Pounds which he had seen in an inn when visiting Anstruther, a seaport town in Fifeshire, sometime in 1841. The story of that picture is itself remarkable.

Some years before John's death, several friends wanted a portrait of the Portsmouth Cobbler but they knew that he would not agree. One of them, Thomas Sheppard, a boot and shoemaker in the High Street, knew of a shoe repairer in Landport named H.S. Sheaf who was something of a local artist and he persuaded him to make a sketch of John in his cobbler's shop surrounded by his children. This was without John's knowledge and when it was completed was greatly admired as a remarkable likeness. Edward Carter bought it for five pounds. *(Versions of which are reproduced on the front cover and page 13)*

No one was very sure what would be the cobbler's reaction, but he was shown into the room where it was on display, he peered at it and made no gesture of recognition other than the comment "There's my cat". A few days later he did comment to a friend that he was glad that "his two queens" Lizzie Lemon and Georgiana Richmond were in the picture.

Soon after he died, and when interest began to develop, Mr. Charpentier, a well known stationer and engraver, made

Dr. Thomas Guthrie 1803 - 1873

lithograph copies of that picture and they sold widely in the town and beyond. It was one of these lithograph copies which found its way to the little fishing port of Anstruther and excited the interest of Dr. Guthrie. He had long been concerned by the large number of destitute and neglected children in our towns and cities who were not reached by the voluntary schools. He found out all he could concerning John Pounds and his work, and was convinced that ragged schools were the answer.

Soon his movement was launched, and it attracted the interest of Lord Shaftesbury, Charles Dickens, Angela Burdett Coutts and many others. John Pounds came to be known in this country and, indeed, in America as the "originator of Ragged Schools" one of the great pioneering bodies which did much to establish universal education.

In 1852, just thirteen years after the death of John Pounds, the movement was so powerful that, having made applications to the Government for a grant, a Committee of the House of Commons was appointed to inquire into the condition of "criminal and destitute juveniles in this country and what changes are desirable in the present treatment, in order to supply industrial training and to combine reformation with the due correction of juvenile crime".

This was a landmark in the development of public policy regarding the welfare and education of juveniles. And so it was that the work of an obscure local cobbler working in that tiny cobbler's shop in Portsmouth had been the inspiration of that public awakening. Of course, John Pounds would have protested that his contribution to it was modest, but secretly he would have been glad that his work had been remembered in such an appropriate way.

It is a pity that the cobbler's shop, where his work was carried on, no longer exists. Yes, there is the John Pounds Community Centre and a former school which bear his name as does one of the wards in a local hospital.

Picture courtesy of Portsmouth Museums & Records Service.

The Chapel in which he worshipped for so many years was destroyed in the blitz on Portsmouth in 1941 and when it was rebuilt in 1956 it became known as the John Pounds Memorial Church with the Memorial Stone a feature of its garden. Now, it is still the Stone which attracts hundreds of visitors. In the summer term children arrive with their notebooks copying the wording on the Memorial Stone. Other visitors, many from America, want to see the lithograph copy of Sheaf's portrait of John Pounds which hangs in the Church Hall and parents come to the church to have their children's Naming Ceremonies.

PORTSMOUTH CITY COUNCIL
JOHN
POUNDS
1766-1839
Shoemender
whose work for the poor of this district inspired the Ragged School Movement is buried in the Memorial Garden

Replica Workshop & Memorial Stone

So he, who lived and worked in obscurity, became the inspiration of a great national movement that is still remembered today over 160 years after his death.

The story of John Pounds has been a source of inspiration to many over the years. It must continue to inspire and encourage others for years to come.

Editor's Notes:

1. The following appeared in the 1966 exhibition programme celebrating the bi-centenary of the birth of John Pounds:

RAGGED SCHOOLS, PORTSMOUTH

There were a number of Ragged Schools and kindred institutions in Portsmouth and the following is, as far as can be ascertained, a complete list:—

Free Ragged School, Richmond Place, Portsea, founded 1849; Highbury Training School, founded 1850; John Pounds Memorial Ragged School, Oyster Street, founded 1860 and the Industrial School with which it was combined from 1875; Ragged School, Kent Street, Portsea; Ragged School, Marylebone Street, Landport, founded 1875 or earlier; Shaftesbury Institute for Poor Lads, Fratton Road; Industrial School, Poor House Lane,; Sunday School, John Pounds' shop, founded 1891; The Insitute, 79, St. Thomas's Street, founded 1898 in connexion with the Independent Chapel; John Pounds Training Home for Girls, founded 1900.

2. *In 2004 a replica of the cobbler's workshop was completed beside the grave of John Pounds in the garden of the Church that was named in his memory. Many of the artefacts and tools in this workshop (many very, very worn and old) were donated by people from all over Britain when they heard that a replica workshop was to be built. This replica is available for educational and community visits and guided talks.*

A Double Tragedy

by Dr Ann Coats, Portsmouth Dockyard Historian.

The tragic events which befell the two John Pounds, father and son, in May 1781.

Dockyard pay books prove incontrovertibly that John Pounds senior and junior both worked in Portsmouth Dockyard in the 1770s and 1780s. The father was a sawyer and his son an apprentice shipwright. John junior was entered on 19 March 1778 as a servant (apprentice) to John Tanner, a Quarter Man Shipwright. Paid 14d a day, John worked 11 days and 19 tides in this quarter, earning wages of 17s 7d and a lodgings allowance of 4d.[3] His master, a senior shipwright, was paid 30d a day, earning £12 7s 6d and a lodgings allowance of 2s 7d.[4] The most valued workers were granted an apprentice and parents paid a premium for their son. The master received the boy's wages and benefited from his labour for seven years, paying him an allowance, sometimes housing and feeding him. As the son of a dockyard worker, John would have been favoured for a place.

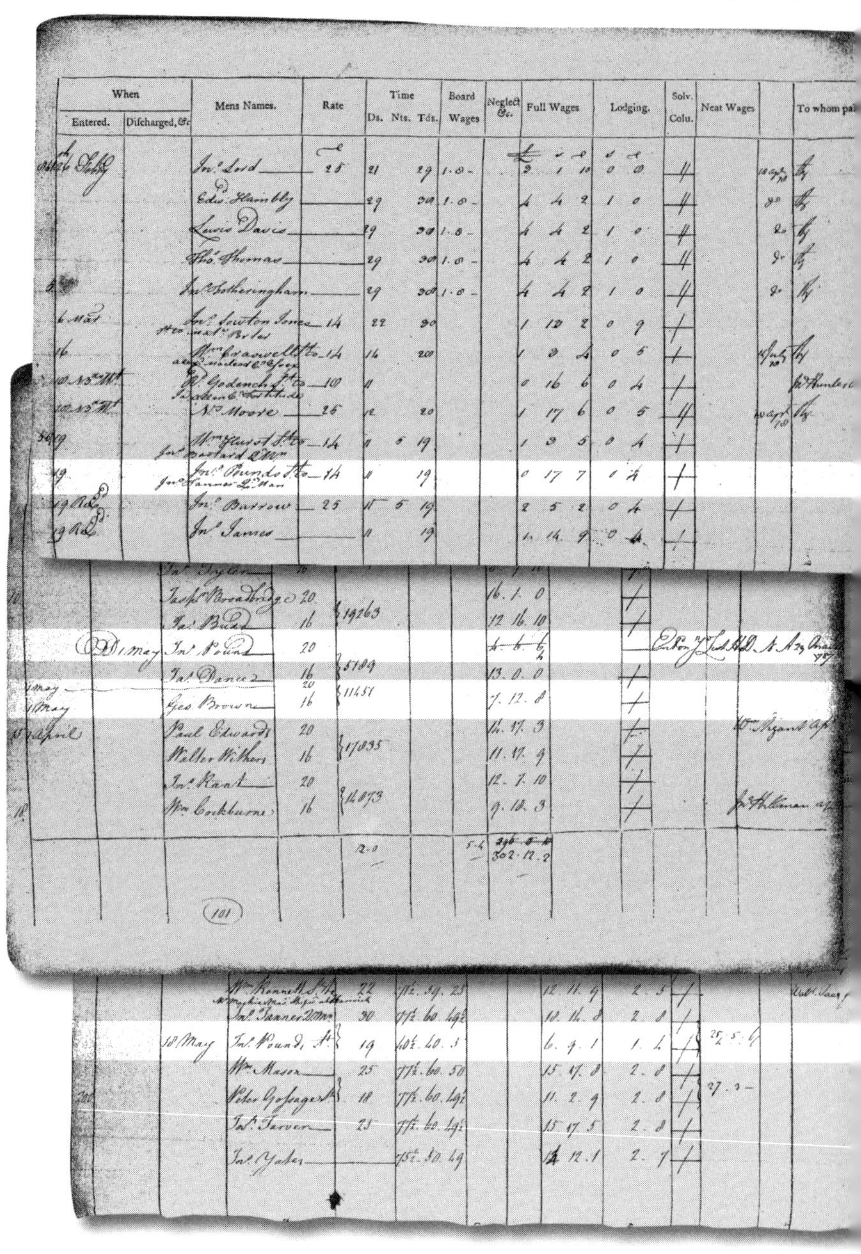

The National Archives: top to bottom: ADM42/1294, part 1, 1778, p.3
ADM42/1297, part 2, 1781, p.1
ADM42/1294, part 2, 1781, p.9.

Being apprenticed to a respected shipwright gave him promotion prospects once qualified, with good pay rates for life. Dockyards retained their own apprentices in cutbacks.

By the end of 1780 John junior's quarterly earnings were £9 19s 4d and by the third quarter his daily rate had risen to 19d a day, showing he was clearly a first-rate apprentice with good prospects.[5] But in April-June 1781 he only worked 40.5 days, 40 nights and 5 tides, earning only £6 9s 1d and lodgings of 1s 4d, because he was discharged on 18 May.[6] In the final quarter Tanner had another apprentice, Benjamin Martell.[7] This may well have been John's relative, as the Portsmouth surgeon George Martell later confirmed that he was a first cousin once removed to John.[8] Sadly, while old shipwrights were frequently retained for their skills, an apprentice needed to be fit and active for a lifetime of heavy physical labour. The dockyard had no obligation to retain John as he had not served his time, and he would not be eligible for a pension. Shipwrights were liable to cut their hamstrings with the adze. Falls from ship into dock were also a risk.

John Pounds senior was a sawyer, the top man working in a sawpit with his partner Joseph Kearley. They sawed wooden planks in a sawpit using a two-handed saw. The irons used to secure the wood were called dogs so the 'underdog' would get sawdust in his eyes. They were sawing around 200 feet of oak a day as a pair. Pounds was paid 20d a day, his wages typically around £16 a quarter. On 8 August 1780 Kearley was discharged and replaced by James Dance.[9]

In the first quarter of 1781 Pounds senior's wages of £16 11s 2d were crossed through, with the comment 'Entered on ye List H. D. S A 29 March 1787.'[10] In the second quarter he was paid £4 6s 6d, crossed through, with the remark 'Discharged Dead 1 May.' On the same day Dance became the top man on 20d a day, with a new partner George Brown.[11] There is no explanation for his wages being crossed through for the last two quarters. Perhaps he was sick before he died, but if he had been absent he would not have been paid. The extra comment (*added later in different handwriting*) suggests he had been recommended for superannuation, a scheme to give old, unfit but deserving workers a pension. In the eighteenth century there was not enough money to pay all those nominated by dockyard officers and many like John Pounds senior died before receiving it.

These stark facts show poignantly that John Pounds was discharged eighteen days after his father's death. We cannot know if grief caused his attention to wander and led to the accident. Through bereavement he had lost an important family connection to the dockyard patronage network; through his accident he lost the support of his master, who could not carry someone who could no longer perform his role.

Charles Dickens and John Pounds

by A J Pointon, Emeritus Professor, University of Portsmouth

It was 1838 before the Portsmouth-born writer Charles Dickens returned to the home town that he had left 23 years before when he was almost three. John Pounds was then 71 years old. Just previously, in early February, Dickens had been visiting the North of England carrying out research for his next novel - Nicholas Nickleby - which was to begin publication in monthly episodes in the April. His subject of research had been the notorious "Yorkshire Schools" that he was determined to expose, reform or close down. His impression of them he left us in his description of Dotheboys Hall and its owner-headmaster Wackford Squeers in the first four episodes of his novel. To those schools, he explained, boys were sent to be isolated from their

Nicholas chastises Squeers for his treatment of Smike

families 250 miles from London with no holidays, poor food, poor treatment and poor education: Dickens may have exaggerated, as a former journalist would, but five years from their exposure they had virtually disappeared. [12;13]

The research that he was to do for his novel in Portsmouth was into the theatre. In the novel, he had Nicholas leave Greta Bridge where Dotheboys Hall was located - after giving Squeers a thrashing - and walk to London, before setting off over London Bridge onto the Portsmouth Road at Southwark with the intention of becoming a sailor. The accidental outcome was that on the way Nicholas would fall in with an actor- manager, Vincent Crummles, and join his company at the Portsmouth Theatre Royal which stood (until it was pulled down in 1854) on the opposite side of the High Street and slightly north from the Unitarian Church that was to become the John Pounds Memorial Church. Given what Dickens had left behind in Yorkshire (and was then writing up for his novel) Dickens was in for a profound and very pleasant surprise.

From his description of Nicholas's arrival in Portsmouth with his companion Smike, the pupil who had run away from his treatment at the hands and cane of Squeers to join Nicholas on the road, it is clear where Dickens walked. He first went to the theatre that he would have seen as a child - at least from the outside - and certainly knew about. He then walked down the High Street, turned right along a short length of St. Mary's Street (now Highbury Street) to St. Thomas's Street where he proceeded south "to the house of Bulph the pilot, who sported a boat-green door." It was there, in his novel, he was to lodge the Crummles family. Leaving Bulph's, with Nicholas and Smike as his imaginary companions, Dickens describes the search for suitable lodgings for them that ended just outside the Portsmouth dockyard gate that his father would have known so well: he found for them "two small rooms up three pair of stairs, or rather two pair and a ladder, at a tobacconist's shop on the Common Hard."

The route he would have taken from St. Thomas's Street to the Hard was along St. Mary's Street where was sited the cobbler's shop of John Pounds which doubled as his school. It is not difficult to imagine Dickens's reaction to the contrast thrust upon him between the neglect he had reported from Greta Bridge and the simple love and dedication that had grown up around John Pounds and those from his Church who had actively supported his work. It may be he had seen John Pounds's workshop before he left Portsmouth in 1815 and heard about him through his father's reminiscences, but here was something quite different.

In 1838 the school had features that may have originally been invented by John Pounds but were now widespread and soon were to become the hall-marks of the Ragged Schools: its existence and methods, and the character and the portrait of its founder were known from south to north of Britain with affection; and Dickens - who talked to everyone - could not have avoided stopping and talking to him there. John Pounds was a focal point of the community, a repository and disseminator of information, as well as being a sidesman at the Unitarian Church for which Dickens had an affection.[14]

Although Dickens did not write about John Pounds and his school directly, he seems to have absorbed the crippled teacher into the melting pot where he kept his characters. Dickens's next novel after *Nicholas Nickleby* was *The Old Curiosity Shop* begun in

Master Humphrey greets Samuel Pickwick

1840.[15] In it the best of all Dickens's schoolmasters was to appear. He referred to him as "the poor schoolmaster", described him as "a pale, simple looking man, of spare and meagre habit". He gave him a stick to lean on and a book to read as he walked. He named him Mr Marton, recalling the medieval name - marteau - for a cobbler's hammer. This was the man who would take in Little Nell and her grandfather when they could go no further, and who would care for her until she died.

The Old Curiosity Shop was published by Dickens in his new journal that was also started in 1840. He called it *Master Humphrey's Clock.* This name he got from the owner of a clock-and-watchmaker's shop opposite the "Kings Head" where he stayed in Barnard Castle while visiting Greta Bridge. The journal's narrator, Master Humphrey, seemingly another echo of John Pounds, described himself as "a misshapen, deformed old man" and explained that he had overcome the initial repulsion of his neighbours so that "the women and children no longer retreated'' and he could say "I never walk abroad but pleasant recognition and smiling faces wait on Master Humphrey."[16]

The coincidences here seem too strange to be coincidences, and one gets another echo of a lingering memory of this good man when, in 1857, Dickens has Little Dorrit go in the evenings for her education with the boys at "Mr Cripples's Academy".

Now, it has been said that the name "Ragged School" was invented in February 1843 when "Field Lane Sabbath School" near Saffron Hill, London used that title when it appealed for funds in *The Times* almost 5 years to the day that Dickens walked past John Pounds's school in 1838. (That advert must have given our author a frison when he remembered he had described Oliver Twist going through Saffron Hill to Fagin's den which was located "in a house in Field Lane") However, it is likely that the title "Ragged School'' had been around some time, applied colloquially or even derogatively to a whole range of schools fashioned along the lines laid down by John Pounds and others: in 1835, the parallel London City Mission had announced that it was for "children raggedly clothed". Here it was formalised with the imprimatur of Britain's leading newspaper.

Dickens, who apparently followed the development of the various schools and was often solicited for his help, suddenly found a great opportunity when he enlisted, indeed was offered, as Micawber might have said, the powerful pecuniary participation of Angela Burdett Coutts, the banking heiress. With Dickens's encouragement, she soon had two major charitable projects: a Home for Homeless Women called Urania Cottage and, on a much larger scale amounting to millions of pounds, funding for the Ragged Schools that Dickens extolled to her in a bundle of letters at the end of 1843. It is no surprise that one of the streets near the "Ragged School Museum" in the East End of London is named Coutts Road, with Copperfield Road alongside it named after Dickens's most autobiographical novel, for he guided the millionairess in her benevolence to those schools until his death in 1870.

Portsmouth in the time of John Pounds (1766 -1839)

Part 2 by Elizabeth Barnes-Downing

The life of John Pounds crossed between two centuries, a 73-year period which ran into the reigns of four successive monarchs of the United Kingdom of Great Britain and (by 1801) Ireland; and 22 offices of Prime Minister (some individuals headed Parliament on a number of occasions). The same period also saw a sea change in economic, scientific and political thought, and in social policy.

The large scale adoption of scientific reasoning and logic by scholars in the eighteenth century influenced by the rationalist, Descartes, and furthered by empiricists, Bacon and then Locke, all from the previous century, challenged traditional religious and philosophical dogma, whilst at the same time establishing a stock of natural scientific knowledge which underpins our current way of life in the western world.

King George III

The 'Age of Enlightenment' in European philosophy was marked by publications by Kant, Voltaire and Rousseau, amongst others. Dr. Adam Smith, the acknowledged father of modern economics, had published *The Wealth of Nations* and Thomas Paine published his pamphlets *The Rights of Man* and *Age of Reason* collectively influencing contemporary thought on the principles of freedom, the free market and supporting non-conformism in religion.

William Smith, the founder of geological science, produced a large scale geological map of Britain in 1815 after twenty years' work surveying and collating geological data, the world's first ever geological survey map of any country. In 1831 Charles Darwin set out on a five year long voyage on The Beagle, studying animal species and communities and in 1839 sketched out his theory on evolution which, many years later, was published in fuller detail and argument, as *The Origin of Species.*

Transformation of social, spiritual and scientific philosophy went hand in hand with changes to the economic infrastructure.

The advance of industrialisation which had begun at the beginning of the 18th century, began slowly to pick up speed around the time of Pounds' birth in 1766, together with changes and improvements in domestic agricultural production. Britain became a dominant trading nation within Europe and overseas, gaining colonies and giving rise to a powerful empire, despite the loss of the American colonies by 1783. The British slave trade – begun in 1698, and heavily campaigned against from 1787[17] – was finally abolished by the Abolition of Slavery Act in 1833.

Adjustments in agricultural techniques, largely the product of improved management, took place during this period, resulting in higher yields in food production, an associated increase in the general population, and greater rationalisation of the rural labour force.[18] The outcome was that large numbers of the rural population were moving into urban areas during this time in search of work.

Social unrest in France at the end of the 18th century resulted in the toppling of the French monarchy and a new social and political order, based on concepts of European enlightenment, liberty, equality and fraternity. Similar events had recently taken place across the Atlantic; the American War of Independence, 1775-1783, resulted in a new constitution and the birth of an independent nation with no allegiance to the British throne.

Although long wars involving the French had been a feature of English life for centuries, it was the bloody emergence of social revolution just a few miles across the English Channel that was particularly feared by the British establishment. Political repression followed in Britain, including changes in the law to prevent public meetings and the formation of trades unions.[19] John Pounds would have been well-informed of these developments, privy as he was to the latest news through his contacts with everyone from the Portsmouth hierarchy to Frank Faulkner, the driver of the Rocket coach to and from London.

During the early years of the 19th century, the rise of Napoleon Bonaparte and his tireless and brutal campaigns to extend his empire within Europe kept the British people and economy occupied, promoted a degree of national pride, and with just a few random breakdowns such as the Spithead Mutiny[20] in 1797, provided sufficient social cohesion to keep the lid on mass unrest. But, when the war ended and its attendant economic downturn emerged, the cumulative effects of various unpopular parliamentary enactments favouring land-owners, such as the 1815 Corn Laws which gave rise to escalating bread prices, led to further civil unrest. Incidents, including the assassination of the British Prime Minister Spencer Perceval in 1812,

Manchester's 'Peterloo' Massacre[21] in 1819, the notorious Cato Street conspiracy[22] of 1820, and the transportation of the Dorset Tolpuddle Martyrs[23] fourteen years later served to confirm the fears of those in government that Britain was on the brink of its own social revolution.[24] In the face of grinding poverty, compassionate humanitarianism, which had become fashionable amongst the rich and powerful, contributed in part to the Reform Bill passed early in 1832.

The Tolpuddle Martyrs
Courtesy of The Tolpuddle Martyrs Museum

By the time John Pounds died in 1839 the foundations of a new Britain had been laid - Queen Victoria was into her second year of what was to be more than sixty years of sovereignty and achievement in terms of social and public health, infrastructure and industry.

Queen Victoria

In sickness and in health

For the ordinary person day to day existence was harsh. There was a mass of illiterate unskilled labour. Free education was unheard of, the concept of organised state education had not arisen, but some limited educational opportunities were provided by church organisations. Even for those few who received a basic education, society was rigidly stratified - prospects were limited, and ambition stifled. Standards of public and private hygiene were poor, food adulteration was practiced on a level that is inconceivable by today's standards, and cooking facilities for the working classes were primitive. Drunkenness was widespread amongst society's poorer classes, subjecting many children to neglect or acts of parental violence. Even young children could be made destitute having been turned out of their homes by their parents and forced to fend for themselves. All this, combined with inadequate clothing, limited the chances of survival of the children of the poor.[1]

The first Public Health Act was not passed until 1848, nine years after John Pounds's death, and a sound understanding of the pathological cause of disease and accompanying changes to town planning were still some years away.[25] Smallpox and typhus were endemic in the poor areas, together with other common diseases such as whooping-cough, measles and scarlet fever. There were sporadic outbreaks of cholera between 1832 and 1866 throughout the heavily populated towns of Britain. During an outbreak in 1848-49 scores of people in the cramped dwellings of Portsmouth died, whereas only two isolated cases were reported in the finer housing of the High Street.[26] In Portsmouth the prison hulks were affected in 1833, prisoners, guards and a naval surgeon died as a result.

Associated with the increasing migration of people from the countryside to towns nationwide was a dramatic expansion in the death rate amongst the urban population, particularly amongst the poor.[27] The cemeteries by this time were grossly inadequate: In Portsmouth, a new burial ground of 4 acres was established in 1831 on London Road, Portsea Island: by 1850 there were over 6,000 graves on this site, and natural springs of a 'distinct dark colour' flowed from the grounds into an open drain in the street. Evidence given in the Rawlinson Report to the Central Board of Health in 1850 described a cellar under a house in the High Street, adjacent to St Thomas's Church, as often overflowing with the 'putrid drainage of the churchyard'. In addition, a nauseating stench inside the church was tracked to 'a decomposing body in a coffin' laid beneath a flagstone. Other reports from the time show that this horrific state of affairs was certainly not unique to Portsmouth.[28]

By contrast, one of the sights pointed out to visitors to Portsmouth was the impressive Haslar Hospital, which could be observed across the harbour in Gosport. This building, completed in 1762, was jointly acclaimed as the first Naval hospital in the country and, with the capacity for 1,500 men, the largest continuous brick building in Europe.[29]

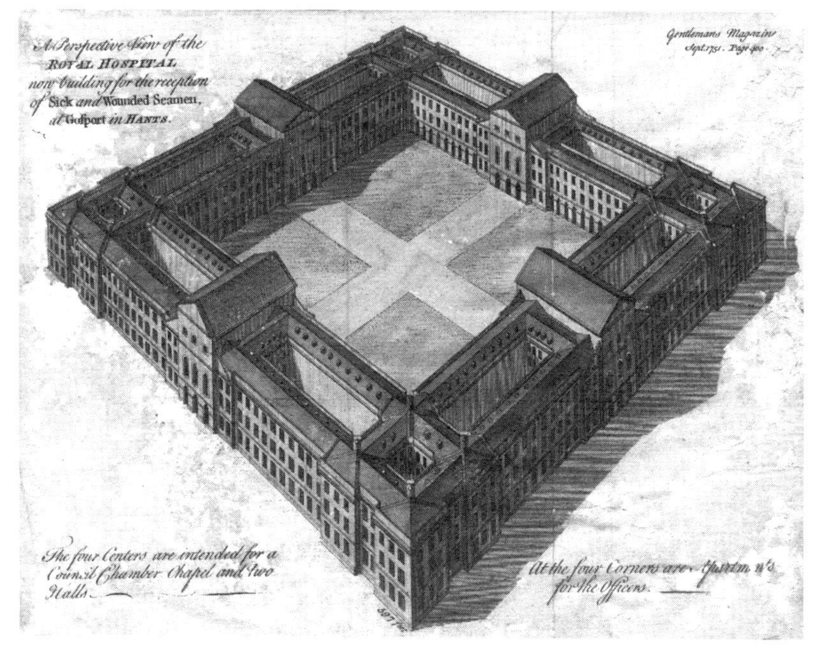

Haslar Plan as published in the Gentleman's Magazine of 1751. Courtesy of Royal Hospital Haslar.

For richer, for poorer

The three centres of activity on Portsea Island during the period were Portsmouth itself, the Royal Naval Dockyard and Portsea, all of which were walled and heavily defended. Outside these on the rest of the Island, which was (and still is) separated from the mainland by a narrow strip of tidal water, there were market gardens, farms and the agricultural communities of Hilsea, Kingston, Copnor, Buckland, Fratton and Milton. The eastern side of the Island was largely marshland under pasture, with the Great Saltings – a redevelopment of the salt industry originating from ancient times.

Salt Barns. Courtesy of Portsmouth in the Past.

Outside Portsmouth's walls to the south-east the land was largely poorly drained marsh, scrub, and gorse - the Little Morass which covered part of Southsea Common and the Great Morass on the central southern shore of the Island. Attempts to drain these areas for building purposes were not successful until the first third of

W Turner of Oxford, Portsmouth Harbour 1813. Picture courtesy of Portsmouth Museums & Records Service.

the nineteenth century. As an indication of the scale of population increase on Portsea Island during the Napoleonic wars, a fashionable and elegant residential suburb began to develop on the better drained areas adjacent to the town's eastern walls. This suburb, named Southsea, provided accommodation for many of the area's nobility and gentry, and from 1830 onwards became an increasingly middle-class satellite of the Dockyard and garrisons. It housed naval and military personnel, retired officers, and their families, and developed into a Victorian seaside attraction. The open expanse of Southsea Common which still contributes to Southsea seafront's distinctiveness today owes itself not only to the earlier dominance of the marshland conditions, but also to the military who maintained control of the area until as recently as 1923. The building line of Southsea's southern development was thereby restrained a long way back from the sea.[30]

As Charles Dickens knew, and later wrote, the best and worst of times could also be found in Portsmouth. It was the flagship base for Great Britain during the war years because of its strategic position opposite the enemy threat in France and its enormous natural harbour with one narrow inlet which made it easy to defend. Ironically, the American war of independence and the French wars heralded a boom period for the economy of Portsmouth. The Royal Navy was largely self-sufficient with regard to capital, naval supplies, ship-building and manufacturing. However, it was a major employer of labour from the neighbouring towns of Portsmouth and Portsea to man these industries within the Portsmouth Dockyard as well as the ships at sea. Significant activities within the town to supply essentials to the navy, its workforce and visitors to the town (from land or sea) included the manufacture of clothing, footwear and brewing.[31;32] Other activities included seaborne trade,[33] hospitality, retailing[26] and prostitution gathered in the area to service a ready market in the naval and military garrisons.

Brunel's Birthplace. Courtesy of Portsmouth in the Past.

Meanwhile, industrialisation, begun in the Midlands and North of England, began to make inroads further south. In the early 19th century a young French engineer named Marc Brunel came with his English wife to live in Portsea, where Isambard Kingdom Brunel, their only son, was born in 1806. Marc, a prolific inventor, was commissioned by the British Government to design and install machinery for the RN Dockyard, Portsmouth, to produce wooden pulley blocks, a task which had been done manually for centuries.

Chubb Family Home.

Several years later, also in Portsea, a locksmith named Jeremiah Chubb designed the detector lock in 1816. The lock mechanism was claimed to be impossible to pick – and had been tested extensively and officially. A convict imprisoned on one of the hulks in Portsmouth harbour also tested it but without success. The detector lock was patented in 1818. In 1824 Jeremiah's brother, Charles, took over the business making further improvements to the lock and taking out subsequent patents. However leaving Portsea behind as an industrial base, he founded a huge factory in London to massproduce Chubb locks a decade later.[34]

After the British victory against Napoleon, firstly at Trafalgar with Admiral Lord Nelson in 1805 and the final defeat at Waterloo with Wellington in 1815, the economy of Britain generally slumped. In towns like Portsmouth with a major defence role, the effect hit hard. At the end of the 18th century, the Dockyard employed more than 4,000 men.[35] For a period of almost thirty years after the end of the Napoleonic wars, the Dockyard activities were reduced[36] and workers were laid off in large numbers. The workforce was reduced from 3,582 men in 1813 to only 1,610 by 1830, and the knock-on effects had a huge impact on the rest of the local economy. This was amplified by the Dockyard's persistence in using unpaid convict labour for heavy labouring and hauling work. The practice began at the turn of the 19th century, replacing paid labourers, carters and their horses.

Crime and Punishment

Socially deviant and criminal behaviour in British society has been described as being rife during this period. In the cramped and squalid towns and cities, where policing was weak or non-existent and traditional communities had been broken down by the rapid economic downturn and movement within the urban population, crime was seen as inevitable and the official response to it was severe. Two hundred and twenty-three offences were listed on the statute books as deserving of the death penalty, which resulted in virtual queues at the gallows and an accompanying undercurrent of social unrest and the risk of revolution. In Newgate, London, it was not uncommon for twenty people sentenced for capital punishment to be hanged in one session.[37]

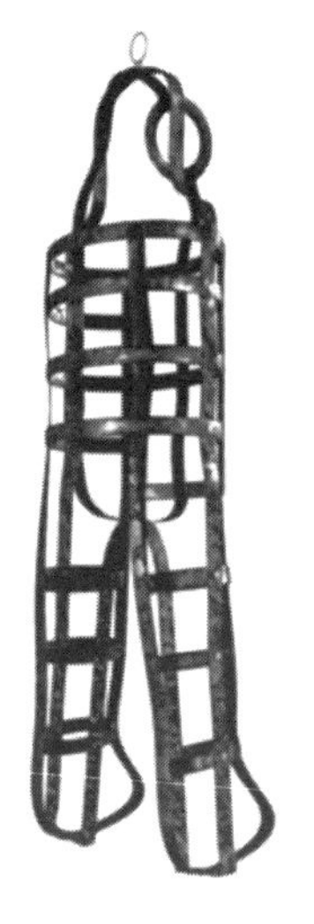

Gibbet irons

In Portsmouth, a scaffold was set up on the seafront at Southsea Common near the current site of Clarence Parade, although executions by hanging could be decreed to take place near the scene of the crime – as in the notorious case of the so-called John the Painter. He was a Scot who was tried by the Winchester Assizes and convicted in 1777 for attempting to burn down the Portsmouth Dockyard one year earlier.[38] He was hanged and his body gibbeted at the entrance to Portsmouth Harbour. This practice of displaying the corpses of criminals to become carrion was widespread, and believed to act as a deterrent for anyone else thinking of perpetrating similar acts.

John the Painter
Picture courtesy of Portsmouth Museums & Records Service.

Petty thieving was rife and the State, represented and administered on a county level by the all powerful Justices of the Peace,[39] treated all brought before them for crimes against property with nearly as much harshness as those found guilty of treason,[40] murder, highway robbery and piracy.

Prison Hulk York, circa 1840. An engraving by E. W. Cooke. *Picture courtesy of Portsmouth Museums & Records Service.*

Children over the age of seven received equally brutal sentences as adults, although very young children convicted of felonies often had their sentences commuted to 'lighter' penalties. First time offenders were generally treated with what, at the time, was considered a degree of leniency. Several weeks' hard labour could be meted out as a sentence for subsequent offenders for such trifling offences as loitering in the street.[1] In capital cases, the death sentence could be substituted with transportation to one of the British colonies for an average of seven years – although only a small percentage of those transported ever came back.

The First Fleet, a total of eleven ships; six convict ships, three store ships and two men-of-war - commanded by Captain Arthur Phillip, left Portsmouth to establish a basic colony in Botany Bay, Australia in 1788. This provided an additional location for transportation after the loss of the American colonies. During the following sixty years, over 800 ships carried more than 160,000 convicts to Australia.[41] Dangerous convicts and those awaiting transportation were held in prison hulks, decommissioned vessels retained in the upper reaches of Portsmouth Harbour for the purpose.

Religion, Dissenters and Local Politics

When it came to matters of belief, significant numbers of the town's civilian population embraced nonconformism, liberal concepts of enlightenment and human rights. Several of the town's mayors and aldermen attended the nonconformist chapel on the High Street, which was founded in 1662 as a dissenter Presbyterian chapel and became the Unitarian chapel in the early 19th century. The 18th century building (pictured opposite) was destroyed in 1941 by an incendiary bomb in World War II. It was rebuilt in 1955/6 on the same site and is still here today.

For years there had been a political power struggle between the Admiralty and the civilian elite for control over Portsmouth's jurisdiction, with the Navy losing. There was liberalism of a sort, fostered by those many in the RN Dockyard and the Town Council who practised nonconformist religions. These were people who supported John Pounds in his egalitarian schooling methods.

Portsmouth and its surrounding areas also held in custody foreign prisoners captured during separate conflicts between Britain, North America and then with France. During the long wars of independence between Britain and North America, warrants were issued in 1777 by His Majesty, King George III for the establishment of two special sites for the imprisonment of captured American rebels. One such prison was situated between Plymouth and Plymouth Dock, in Devon. The second was Forton

one mile northwest of Gosport on the peninsula adjacent to Portsea Island, which was designed to accommodate up to 2,000 detainees. American prisoners would usually pass through Portsmouth on their way to Forton. They would be examined by magistrates or Admiralty officials prior to being charged with treason against His Majesty – from there they could be observed by Portsmouth citizens being led to the Gosport ferry to be committed to Forton Prison.

The Reverend Thomas Wren, minister at the High Street nonconformist chapel when John Pounds was a child, sought to mitigate their distress from alleged mistreatment through donations of money, improved food supplies, clothing and personal comforts. At times he subsidised this from his own pocket, together with the provision of schooling. From this contact, and through his own feelings about the American war, he also became a source of news and reports, and messages, from the outside world, and it is likely that his support helped to reduce the number of prisoners who might otherwise have abandoned the patriotic cause and volunteered for the service of King George III simply

Sir John Carter. Picture courtesy of Portsmouth Museums & Records Service.

to escape the monotony and discomfort of detainment. As the war with America progressed The Reverend Thomas Wren risked severe penalties for his secret and illicit activities in concealing and leading escapees from Forton to Portsmouth and onward to London through various pro-American channels.

Sir John Carter, Mayor of Portsmouth on eight occasions, and a member of one of the most politically active families in the town at the time, lived on the High Street opposite the nonconformist chapel, and his strong opposition to the American war was well known. Although no written evidence has been uncovered to prove that Carter and his political associates were actual accessories to the sanctuary and support of American escapees, their involvement with The Reverend Thomas Wren and proximity to the chapel does strongly implicate them.[42] In 1780 Wren received a letter from Benjamin Franklin recognising his endeavours for the American cause of Independence, and three years later he was awarded an honorary doctorate by the Presbyterian College of New Jersey. He never actually visited America and, apart from travelling from time to time to the area of his birth in the Lake District, North-West England, remained at the High Street Chapel until his death in October 1787.

Communication and Transport

Because of its military significance, Portsmouth was at the centre of communications. The installation of the shutter telegraph in 1796 had reduced the timc needed to send a message from Portsmouth to the Admiralty in London from many hours (via road) to ten minutes. The transmission of messages could take place only in daytime, with accompanying clear weather. However it was a substantial improvement over the simple signal of a burning beacon which had been used to herald the Spanish Armada more than two centuries before. Relayed short messages by line of sight conveyed military orders and had much to do with the timely reduction of the Spithead Mutiny.

Shutter Telegraph. Picture courtesy of Portsmouth Museums & Records Service.

Portsmouth's overriding reputation is based upon its long Naval history. But the importance of merchant shipping to the town must not be overlooked. Five main activities took place by sea – domestic coastal trade, foreign trade, naval and military, fishing and smuggling.[33]

Coach & Horses outside The George Hotel , High Street, Old Portsmouth
Courtesy of Portsmouth in the Past.

For transporting dispatches, non-military messages, convicted prisoners for deportation, servicemen and civilians to Portsmouth, a thriving coach trade had built up. As mentioned earlier, the Rocket was one of these coaches, together with the Royal Mail, Defiance, Tantivy, Star of Brunswick, Celerity, and the Royal Blue. It has been estimated that for a period there were between eighty and a hundred coach services running between London and Portsmouth every week, at half-hourly intervals throughout the week-day. Other routes, including Brighton, Bristol, Chichester, Oxford and Winchester were also served from Portsmouth.[26] The 'golden age of coaching' came at the end of the life of John Pounds and continued for nearly a decade after, before being replaced swiftly by the steam train.

Milton Lock, courtesy Portsmouth Museum and Records Service

A similar fate befell the canal which was built to allow goods brought via the coast to Langstone Harbour, east of the village of Milton, with the potential to be transported cheaply and efficiently to the eastern outskirts of Landport. Regrettably it never made a profit. The canal has now vanished, replaced by Goldsmith Avenue along part of its route.

For successful fast travel, the state of the roads was a big issue. The main road between Portsmouth and London at that time had three turnpikes which funded the improvement of the road surface, enabling stage coaches to travel at relatively high speed, but with relatively little comfort for the passengers. The risks from highwaymen and vagabonds had been so significant that it was also known as the Road of Assassination.[43] It is said that people often made their wills before making the journey. But even as late as the 1820's, other life-threatening possibilities were still present. The steep slopes and sharp corners of the road at Butser Hill resulted in many overturned coaches.

Lurching down the notorious slope of the chalk downlands, the travellers on the outside would get an unparalleled view of the Island: the gigantic natural harbour, moored ships and hulks to the right; Portsea Island in front with Portsmouth at its tip obscured by a forest of ship masts; the Isle of Wight visible across Spithead and Langstone Harbour to the left. To the far distant left, the faint spire of Chichester Cathedral would be seen, while to the far right a distant strip of water marked the Solent, leading to the rival commercial port of Southampton. The pleasant country air rising up the hill face would contain just a hint of what smells were to come.

The stench of civilisation was so pervasive at the time that most writers of the day appear to have decided that comment was superfluous apart from in extreme cases. In spite of the fact that Portsmouth's High Street had been paved since 1770, there

L. Garneray, Prison Hulks in Portsmouth Harbour, c.1810. Picture courtesy of Portsmouth Museums & Records Service.

were still no provisions made in the town for sanitation other than contracts made with 'scavengers' to clear the 'night soil' (human and animal waste) from the streets, gutters and pits. This would be used for spreading on the farmland outside the town walls and on the common fields but the presence of a night curfew created logistical problems for the night soil men as well as making life difficult for the residents.

The smell of open drains, street soil and effluvia from rotting material in the nearby Camber was sufficiently extreme for the Point to be nicknamed 'Spice Island' – a name still used today, although its ironic origins are less well-known. The waste and rubbish collected by the town's scavengers was stored against the wall of the Quay Gate, prior to being sold on, but the Garrison Commander-in-Chief, General Sir William Pitt, strongly objection to this practice in 1799 and it was stopped.

Quay Gate. Picture courtesy of Portsmouth Museums & Records Service.

The scavengers were able to make a living clearing Portsmouth's street dung left by horses and selling it for use as agricultural fertiliser. In 1808 one and a quarter wagonloads per acre were distributed on local fields.[44] The probable result was crops of the sort noted with approbation by William Cobbett in 1823. His *Rural Rides* observations on Portsdown Hill noted the dimensions and the produce: *"The hill is eight miles long, and about three-fourths of a mile high, beginning at the road that runs along at the foot of the hill...... From Bedhampton, which lies at the eastern end of the hill, to Fareham, which is at the western end of it, you have brought under your eye not less*

View from Portsdown Hill 1823. Picture courtesy of Portsmouth Museums & Records Service.

than eight square miles of corn fields, with scarcely a hedge or ditch of any consequence, and being, on average, from twenty to forty acres each in extent......The corn under the hill is as good as I ever saw it, except in the year 1813. No beans here. No peas. Scarcely any oats. Wheat, barley, and turnips...... In looking at these crops, one wonders whence are to come the hands to clear them off."

The answer lay in the cheap labour to be found in the area, which was also prone to remove crops from local fields. 'Scrumping' (stealing apples) was a high risk activity for little boys, some of whom received 'hard labour' sentences for their pains. Poor wages in England, together with increasing farm mechanisation, eventually led to agricultural riots in 1830 which spread from Kent. In Hampshire these resulted in destruction of farm machinery and arson in local areas around Portsea Island and widespread protest within.[44]

So, as the London coach rolled across the bridge onto the Island, it would not be surprising if the arriving passengers had mixed feelings about the prospect that awaited them. The risks of the road journey were shortly to be replaced by the risks of the town experience. Leaving the countryside, the coach passed close to the superior overspill housing at Mile End Road, one of which was the family home and birthplace of Charles Dickens. This area was free of the restrictions of space suffered by those within the town walls. Passing the imposing walls of both the RN Dockyard and the neighbouring town of Portsea, on the right, the huge Landport Gate gave entry to Portsmouth. This was the largest of the town's five gates, designed to keep people in their place, in or out, and to impose a measure of order into the lives of the inhabitants.

Arriving before the military curfew (which ran from midnight until four in the morning) and rumbling through the crowded streets, at least some of the passengers must have been apprehensive as they recalled the contrast between the peaceful country scenes they had so recently left and the turmoil of the Portsmouth streets.

Bridging town and country, the annual Fair brought yet another dimension to town life and its heady mix of smells, poverty, wealth, drunkenness and liveliness. Visitors in mid-July would

Landport Gate. Picture courtesy of Portsmouth in the Past.

have experienced the Free Mart Fair, a local event which was set out along the length of the High Street and which lasted for fifteen consecutive days. It had been in existence for almost six hundred years, but after much complaint and increasing protest from the respectable inhabitants concerning the event's worsening drunkenness, noise, disorderly, 'immoral' and criminal activities, it was finally abolished in 1847.[45]

Looking North along High Street. Picture courtesy of Portsmouth in the Past.

Passing down the High Street visitors could note the fine modern brick facades which had recently replaced, either partially or completely, the timber buildings from earlier times. At the top of the street, with the exception of the Theatre Royal, the buildings were magnificent residences for the local gentry and middle-classes, a few of which are still standing despite extensive enemy action in the 20th century. Passing the nonconformist chapel, the stretch beyond St. Mary's Street (now Highbury Street) was largely retail, with establishments of such high quality that its reputation as a shopping centre was rated the highest in the country outside London. This reputation belied the conditions of the shop workers who commonly worked for fifteen hours a day, six days a week.[26]

High Street houses. Picture courtesy of Portsmouth in the Past.

Further down the street was St Thomas's Church, now the Cathedral, which could be seen behind a row of contemporary houses, and the Market House and Town Hall in the middle of the roadway.

King James Gate from Point. Picture courtesy of Portsmouth Museums & Records Service.

In between the shops were some banks, and interspersed throughout this commercial section of the street were the town's better inns and taverns. At the lower end of the street was another stone gateway linked to the town walls, which separated the respectable townsfolk from the disreputable activities of Broad Street and The Point.

Portsmouth Point. A caricature by Thomas Rowlandson. Picture courtesy of Portsmouth Museums & Records Service.

Theatre Royal High Street. Picture courtesy of Portsmouth Museums & Records Service.

Just around the corner from the Theatre Royal, and the barracks in the High Street, at the top of Penny Street was the Sessions House - where the prisoners were tried and the Borough Gaol built in 1808. It housed committed debtors, naval deserters and 'disorderly women'.[46]

At the end of their journey passengers made their various ways to destinations according to their means and inclinations. Major inns and taverns on the lower end of the High Street included the George Hotel and the Fountain (both patronised by British and European elite), the Dolphin, the Wellington, the Parade Coffee House and Hotel ("Neale's"), the Three Tuns, and The Crown. The less attractive parts of the town contained many establishments and lodgings catering for those with thinner purses.[47]

John Pounds made it his business to be well-informed about current affairs, people and events. An evening scene outside the coaching inns would often have included two people aware of all that town and country had to offer, a bent old man, John Pounds, talking to Frank Faulkner, the coach driver of the Rocket.

Bath Square. Picture courtesy of Portsmouth in the Past.

A Minister's Recollections of John Pounds

John Pounds was an intuitive and engaging teacher to hundreds of vagabond children. He taught them what they really wanted to know in a way they really wanted to learn while also feeding, clothing and caring for their many ills and continuing his business as a cobbler.

We are fortunate to have verbatim examples of some of his lessons recorded by the Reverend Henry Hawkes, minister for much of the time at the High Street Chapel. His book "Recollections of John Pounds" published by Williams and Norgate in 1884 includes the following examples.

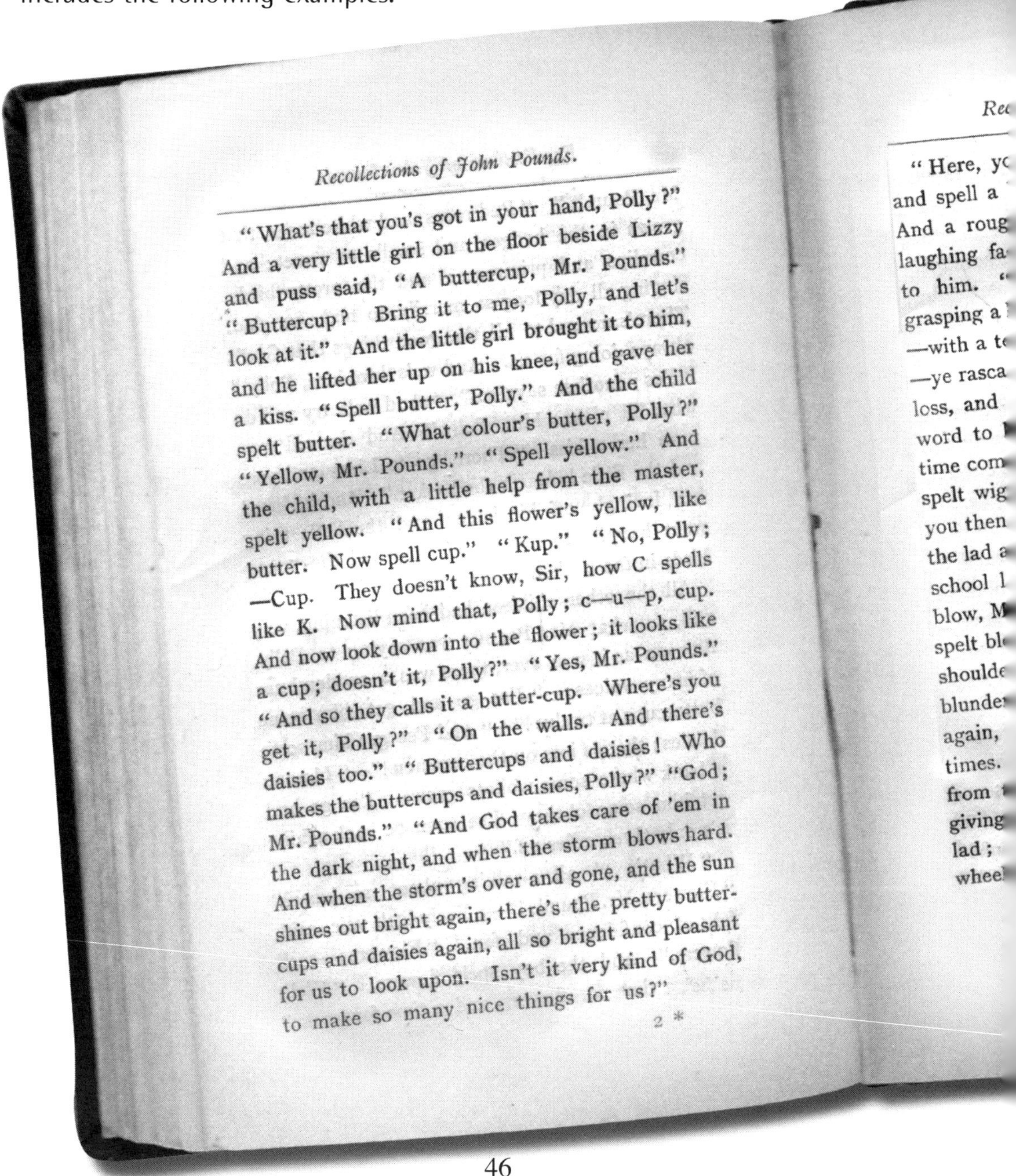

Recollections of John Pounds.

"What's that you's got in your hand, Polly?" And a very little girl on the floor beside Lizzy and puss said, "A buttercup, Mr. Pounds." "Buttercup? Bring it to me, Polly, and let's look at it." And the little girl brought it to him, and he lifted her up on his knee, and gave her a kiss. "Spell butter, Polly." And the child spelt butter. "What colour's butter, Polly?" "Yellow, Mr. Pounds." "Spell yellow." And the child, with a little help from the master, spelt yellow. "And this flower's yellow, like butter. Now spell cup." "Kup." "No, Polly; —Cup. They doesn't know, Sir, how C spells like K. Now mind that, Polly; c—u—p, cup. And now look down into the flower; it looks like a cup; doesn't it, Polly?" "Yes, Mr. Pounds." "And so they calls it a butter-cup. Where's you get it, Polly?" "On the walls. And there's daisies too." "Buttercups and daisies! Who makes the buttercups and daisies, Polly?" "God; Mr. Pounds." "And God takes care of 'em in the dark night, and when the storm blows hard. And when the storm's over and gone, and the sun shines out bright again, there's the pretty butter-cups and daisies again, all so bright and pleasant for us to look upon. Isn't it very kind of God, to make so many nice things for us?"

2 *

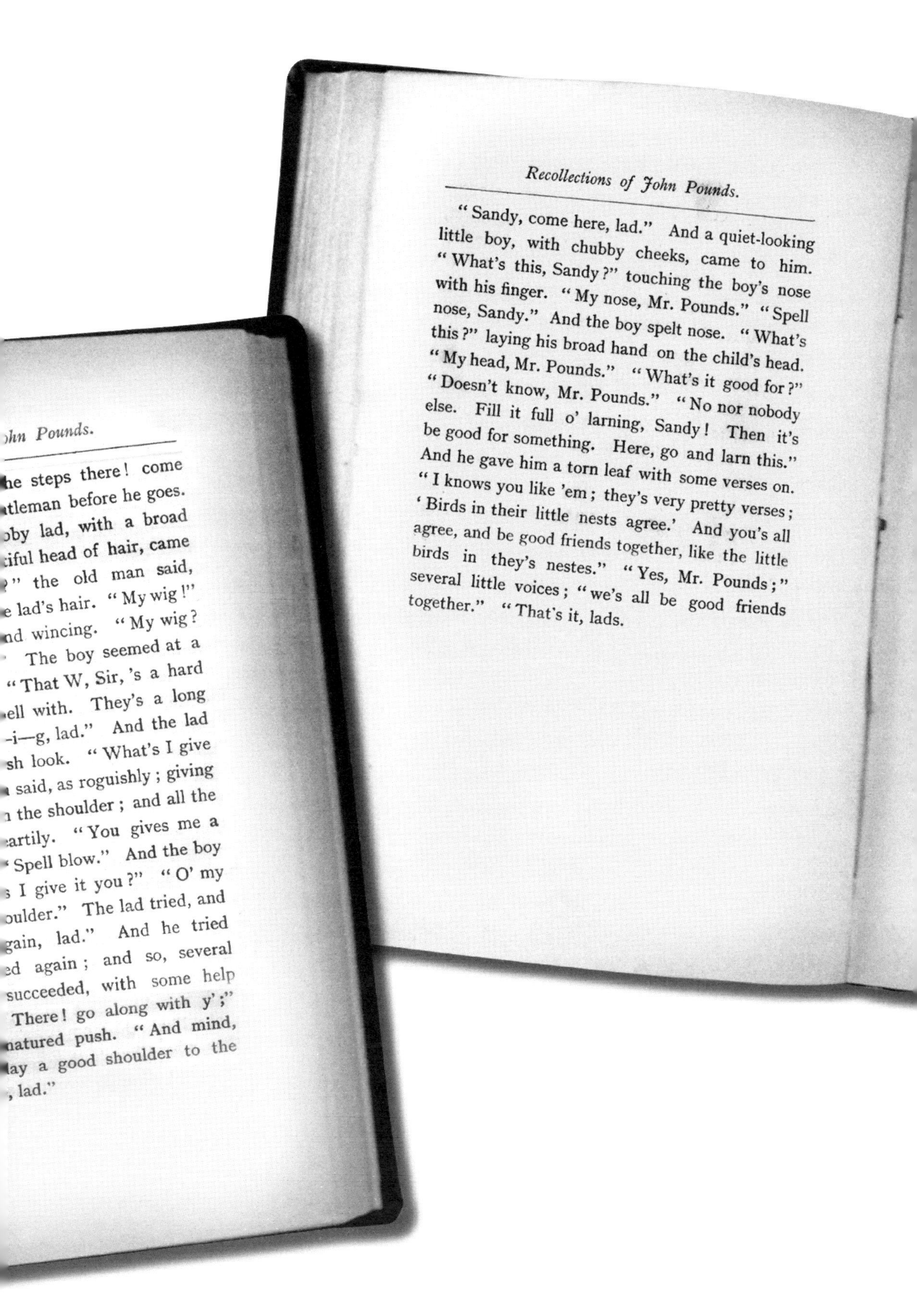
ohn Pounds.

he steps there! come
tleman before he goes.
bby lad, with a broad
tiful head of hair, came
?" the old man said,
e lad's hair. "My wig!"
nd wincing. "My wig?
The boy seemed at a
"That W, Sir, 's a hard
ell with. They's a long
-i—g, lad." And the lad
sh look. "What's I give
said, as roguishly; giving
the shoulder; and all the
artily. "You gives me a
Spell blow." And the boy
I give it you?" "O' my
oulder." The lad tried, and
gain, lad." And he tried
ed again; and so, several
succeeded, with some help
There! go along with y';"
natured push. "And mind,
lay a good shoulder to the
, lad."

Recollections of John Pounds.

"Sandy, come here, lad." And a quiet-looking little boy, with chubby cheeks, came to him. "What's this, Sandy?" touching the boy's nose with his finger. "My nose, Mr. Pounds." "Spell nose, Sandy." And the boy spelt nose. "What's this?" laying his broad hand on the child's head. "My head, Mr. Pounds." "What's it good for?" "Doesn't know, Mr. Pounds." "No nor nobody else. Fill it full o' larning, Sandy! Then it's be good for something. Here, go and larn this." And he gave him a torn leaf with some verses on. "I knows you like 'em; they's very pretty verses; 'Birds in their little nests agree.' And you's all agree, and be good friends together, like the little birds in they's nestes." "Yes, Mr. Pounds;" several little voices; "we's all be good friends together." "That's it, lads.

Appendices

John Pounds Trust

Registered Charity 1083234

Soon after John Pounds death in 1839 a group of local Portsmouth ladies decided to continue his work of caring for unwanted and neglected children. With the help of the Carter family, distinguished in Portsmouth over many years and great supporters of John Pounds work, a house was acquired and a few girls were given a home and the opportunity to train as domestic servants. Soon a larger house was found in Kent Road, Southsea where the good work continued for many years. Sadly this house was lost in World War II bombing raids in 1941.

At the end of the war compensation was received for the loss of the house from the War Commissioners. This money lay idle until 1956 when The Rev. John Sturges was invited to use the money to perpetuate the memory of John Pounds. In 1957 he established a Trust to distribute the income from this investment to assist local school children from poor homes with their studies. For over forty-five years the John Pounds Trust has fulfilled this role, distributing thousands of pounds to hundreds of Portsmouth children using interest from the invested income supplemented by donations and fund-raising.

John Pounds of Portsmouth Heritage Appeal

Registered Charity 1074479

The late Reverend John Sturges spent much of his life researching local history and promoting the life and work of John Pounds. He concluded, as many had done before him, that the value of John Pounds contribution is timeless. A poor self-educated crippled man dedicating his life to care for children who were going to ruin on the streets of Portsmouth, and the development of a system of schooling that met their needs was of considerable benefit to society. In this context their needs were many – food, warmth, shelter, love, values, elementary education and, subsequently, work. John Pounds system, or model, was the first Ragged School that met the 'whole' needs of the pupils and would be reproduced across the nation following his death.

John Sturges felt passionately about re-creating John Pound's home and workshop. To this end he started accumulating funds in 1990 and this led to the formation of The John Pounds of Portsmouth Heritage Appeal in 1998. With the help of fundraising and sponsors sufficient money was amassed for construction of the replica Workshop based on architectural drawings made by city engineers of the original building prior to its loss. Work began in 2002 and the replica, within the grounds of the John Pounds Memorial Church, was formally opened in 2004. Sadly John Sturges did not see his vision become reality as he passed away in 1998.

The intent is to make the replica workshop a focal point for local history and sociological studies covering the late Georgian/early Victorian period with particular emphasis on the Ragged School model that John Pounds developed, how it contributed to the welfare of hundreds of local children and, following formation of the Ragged School Union, to hundreds of thousands across the country.

References and Notes

1 Mrs Jean Stanford and Professor A.Temple Patterson. The condition of the children of the Poor in mid-Victorian Portsmouth. The Portsmouth Papers, No.21, March 1974, Portsmouth City Council.

2 Grant Uden (1969) British Ships and Seamen. A short history in two books. Book Two, The Seamen. Macmillan St Martin's Press.

3 The National Archive, ADM42/1294 part 1 Portsmouth Dockyard Extraordinary Paybook, 1778, p.36. Night: five hours' overtime for a day's pay; tide: 1.5 hours overtime for shipwrights; a lodgings allowance was paid to valued workers such as shipwrights, but not to sawyers.

4 The National Archives, ADM42/1294 part 1 Portsmouth Dockyard Extraordinary Paybook, 1778, p.14.

5 The National Archives, ADM42/1296 part 4 Portsmouth Dockyard Extraordinary Paybook, 1780, p.9

6 The National Archives, ADM42/1297 part 2 Portsmouth Dockyard Extraordinary Paybook, 1781, p.9.

7 The National Archives, ADM42/1297 part 4, Portsmouth Dockyard Extraordinary Paybook, 1781, p.8.

8 Henry Hawkes (1884) Recollections of John Pounds, Williams and Norgate, p.222

9 The National Archives, ADM42/1294 part 1, Portsmouth Dockyard Extraordinary Paybook, 1778, p.100; ADM42/1295 part 1, 1779, p.99; ADM42/1296 part 1, 1780, p.105; ADM42/1296 part 3, p.100; ADM42/1296 part 4, p.98

10 The National Archives, ADM42/1297 part 1, Portsmouth Dockyard Extraordinary Paybook, 1781, p.103.

11 The National Archives, ADM42/1297 part 2, Portsmouth Dockyard Extraordinary Paybook, 1781, p.101.

12 C. Dickens, Nicholas Nickleby (1839).

13 The Dickension, 55, Spring, 1959, "Dickens and the Ragged Schools".

14 C. Dickens, American Notes (1842).

15 C. Dickens, The Old Curiosity Shop (1840).

16 C. Dickens, Master Humphreys Clock, Volumes I to IV (1840).

17 Dr John Oldfield (2001). British Anti-slavery. Society and Culture. Protest and Reform. BBC History website. http://www.bbc.co.uk/history/society_culture/protest_reform/antislavery_01.shtml

18 Mark Overton (2002). Agricultural Revolution in England 1500 – 1850. Society and Culture. Industrialisation. BBC History website. http://www.bbc.co.uk/history/society_culture/industrialisation/agricultural_revolution_05.shtml

19 Dr Myna Trustram (2001). Banners of the British Labour Movement. Society and Culture. Protest and Reform. BBC History website. http://www.bbc.co.uk/history/society_culture/protest_reform/banners_01.shtml

20 Spithead Mutiny: A month-long open revolt by the naval rank and file took place in Portsmouth in Spring 1797. The elected representatives of 16 ships tried to negotiate peacefully with the Admiralty over the low pay and harsh living conditions on board. Talks deteriorated, resulting in minor violence between the mutineers and the authorities, and the deaths of three sailors. Escalation of violence was stemmed in part to the swift, sensible action of the civilian mayor of Portsmouth, Sir John Carter. Overall the men's action was successful and most of their aims were achieved, including a request for a Royal Pardon to avoid reprisals from the authority.

21 Peterloo Massacre: Fears that a huge rally organised by a radical group of parliamentary reformers at St Peter's Field in Manchester on August 16 1819 might end in a riot led to a heavy-handed solution by local magistrates. Several hundred troops, including cavalry, infantry and artillery men were gathered, positioned and sent in to disperse the crowd. An eyewitness account describes the cavalry cutting swathes through the unarmed and densely packed crowd of men, women and children with their sabres, killing eleven people and injuring about 400.

22 Cato Street Conspiracy: The name given to an attempt in February 1820 by a group of revolutionaries to murder all the British cabinet ministers and overthrow the government. The plot was intercepted and foiled, and those involved were arrested. Eleven men were subsequently charged with high treason; of these five were hanged, and five others had their sentences commuted to transportation for life.

23 Tolpuddle Martyrs: Six farm labourers in Tolpuddle, Dorset who had established a workers' union were arrested on trumped up charges and, through a rigged trial at Dorchester Assizes in March 1834, were sentenced to seven years' transportation to Australia: James Brine, James Hammett, James Loveless, John Standfield and Thomas Standfield were sent to New South Wales, and George Loveless, whose transportation was delayed by illness was sent to Tasmania. This action by the authorities was a blatant attempt to suppress trades unions in an attempt to maintain the status quo – the legal punishment applied to the men was described as not so much a punishment upon the offenders themselves but to provide an example and a warning to the working classes in general. A massive public outcry ensued which resulted in the men being granted a Royal Pardon, however it took many months before the instructions for their release were received by the Australian authorities and another two years before the men were brought back home.

24 Professor Eric Evans (2002) British Revolution in the Early 19th Century: How Close? Society and Culture. Protest and Reform. BBC History website. http://www.bbc.co.uk/history/society_culture/protest_reform/revolution_03.shtml

25 S Martin Gaskell (1983). Building Control. National legislation and the introduction of local bye-laws in Victorian England. National Statutes and the Local Community. British Association for Local History.

26 John Webb, MA, FRHistS. An Early Victorian Street, The High Street, Old Portsmouth. The Portsmouth Papers, No. 26. March 1977.

27 Robert Rawlinson, with an introduction by Audrey Coney (1991). Ormskirk Board of Health Report, 1850. Lancashire County Books.

28 John G. Avery (2001). The Cholera Years: An account of the choldera outbreaks in our ports, towns and villages. Beech Books, Southampton, Hampshire.

29 Navy News (2003). Haslar Hospital Celebrates 250 years. http://www.navynews.co.uk/articles/2003/0310/0003101302.asp

30 Dr R.C.Riley, BSc (Econ), The Growth of Southsea as a Naval Satellite and Victorian Resort. The Portsmouth Papers No.16. July 1972. Portsmouth City Council.

31 R.C.Riley, BSc (Econ), PhD. The Industries of Portsmouth in the Nineteenth Century. The Portsmouth Papers, No.25. July 1976. Portsmouth City Council.

32 Philip Eley. Portsmouth Breweries 1492-1847. The Portsmouth Papers, No. 51, March1988. Portsmouth City Council.

33 Dr James H. Thomas. The Seaborne Trade of Portsmouth 1650-1800. The Portsmouth Papers, No. 40, September 1984. Portsmouth City Council.

34 Anthony Triggs. (1999). Portsmouth First. Halsgrove.

35 Alastair Geddes. Portsmouth during the Great French Wars 1770-1800. The Portsmouth Papers No. 9. March 1970, reprinted 1980. Portsmouth City Council.

36 R.C.Riley, BSc (Econ), PhD. The Evolution of the Docks and Industrial Buildings in Portsmouth Royal Dockyard 1698-1914. The Portsmouth Papers, No. 44, November 1985. Portsmouth City Council.

37 Birkett, N. (1951). The Newgate Calendar. The Folio Society, St James's, London.

38 Neil L. York. Burning the Dockyard: John the Painter and the American Revolution. The Portsmouth Papers, No. 71, March 2001, Portsmouth City Council.

39 Sir Thomas Skyrme (1991) History of the Justices of the Peace. Volume II England 1689-1989. Barry Rose and the Justice of the Peace, Chichester.

40 Treason is a generic name for crimes of disloyalty against the State or against one's lawful superiors. In Britain, during the period covered by this article, high treason included counterfeiting of money, and petty treason included the murder of a husband by a wife. It was not until 1786 that a Bill was brought in by William Wilberforce to bring an end to the burning to death of women found guilty of petty treason.

41 James H. Thomas, BA, PLD FRHistS. Portsmouth and First Fleet 1786 - 1787. The Portsmouth Papers, No. 50, April 1987. Portsmouth City Council.

42 Sheldon S. Cohen. Thomas Wren – Portsmouth's Patron of American Liberty. The Portsmouth Papers, No. 57, March 1991. Portsmouth City Council.

43 Buriton Heritage Bank (2002). Information Sheet No.12. Local roads, stage coaches and highwaymen (March 2002). http://www.buriton.org.uk/bhb/infosheet12.htm

44 Suzanne Shuttleworth. Farms and Market Gardens on Portsea Island 1770 - 1880. The Portsmouth Papers, No. 61, July 1993. Portsmouth City Council.

45 John Webb, MA, FRHistS. Portsmouth Free Mart Fair, The Last Phase 1800-1847. The Portsmouth Papers, Issue No.35. March 1982. Portsmouth City Council.

46 Pat Thompson (1980). Portsmouth Borough Gaol in the Nineteenth Century. The Portsmouth Papers, No.33, September 1980. Portsmouth City Council.

47 R.C.Riley, BSc (Econ), PhD & Philip Eley BSc. Public Houses and Beerhouses in Nineteenth Century Portsmouth. The Portsmouth Papers, No.38, December 1983. Portsmouth City Council.

Additional Reading

Margaret J. Hoad (1973). Portsmouth - As others have seen it. Part II 1790-1900. Portsmouth Papers, Issue No. 20, November 1973. Portsmouth City Council.

Edward Carson (1974). Smugglers and Revenue Officers in the Portsmouth area in the Eighteenth Century - as shown in Customs Records. Portsmouth Papers, Issue No. 22, July 1974. Portsmouth City Council.

Henry Hawks (1884). Recollections of John Pounds. Williams and Norgate.

R. Everett Jayne (1925). The Story of John Pounds. The Epworth Press.

Credits

Barnardo's Image Archive.

Portsmouth Museum and Records Service for invaluable support and images as credited in the text.

Haslar Royal Hospital, Gosport, Hampshire.

Portsmouth in the Past by William Gates including images by Martin Snape.

Patricia Isted, Secretary of John Pounds of Portsmouth Heritage Appeal, for additional research.

Henry Hawkes for his detailed account of John Pounds life and work entitled "Recollections of John Pounds".